To my mom, Arzina, my sister, Farah and my brother, Arif. Thank you for always allowing my dreams to come true, I love you!

To the BC Children's Hospital – Thank you for saving my life!

In loving memory of my dad, Nazir

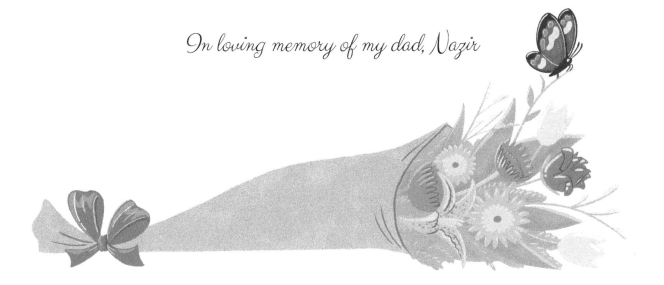

Tellwell Talent
www.tellwell.ca

ISBN
978-0-2288-7077-7 (Hardcover)
978-0-2288-7078-4 (Paperback)

Sophie's Story: I Have Cancer

Safia (Sophie) Dhalla

Illustrated by: Sami Shahin

Hi my name is Sophie and I'm 4 years old. Right now, I live at Children's Hospital and I have cancer.

Cancer is something that makes you really, really sick and you have to stay at the hospital until you are better.

All the doctors and nurses here are so nice. They are always smiling at me and cheering me up when I feel sad, but most importantly they make me feel better when I am feeling sick. They tell me how strong and brave I am.

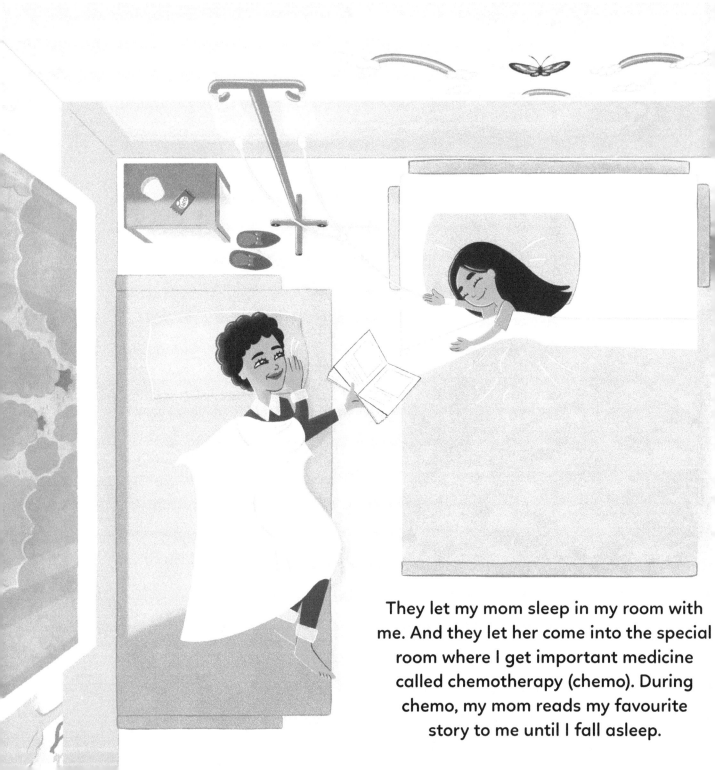

They let my mom sleep in my room with me. And they let her come into the special room where I get important medicine called chemotherapy (chemo). During chemo, my mom reads my favourite story to me until I fall asleep.

Chemotherapy is a very strong medicine. It is making my hair fall out now and I look a little different than I did before. All the other children and my friends here look like me too. This also means we get to wear some pretty cool hats to keep our heads warm.

I am so lucky my family comes to visit me very often. And sometimes they bring me special treats like chicken nuggets and fries and my favourite...chocolate. We also play games together or go on walks around the hospital. Sometimes my dad even takes me to the hospital gift shop to pick out my own special treat.

I have this machine called an IV that comes with me everywhere I go. Sometimes I wish I didn't have it, but I know it is helping me get better and stronger. It also comes with me to the playroom.

I LOVE THE PLAYROOM! It has so many different toys and games. My favourite toy is the green ride-on tractor. This is my favourite place in the hospital because I get to see all my friends who are living at the hospital too. AND sometimes I even get to bring my brother and sister with me.

My hair is growing back and I'm feeling better after being in the hospital for a long time. I get to go home now and the IV stays at the hospital to help other children get better and stronger. I still have to come and visit the hospital often, so the doctors and nurses can make sure I'm feeling better and getting stronger.

I now get to go to the school close to my house. I missed some
Preschool and Kindergarten because I was living at the hospital, but
now I am a big Grade 1 girl. I can't wait to learn how to read and write
and make some new friends. I think I want to be a teacher one day.

I am now 8 years old and guess what? My cancer is GONE! I had to visit the hospital every month to get blood tests to check if the cancer was out of my body. The doctors and nurses did it! They made me feel better after being really sick.

I am now in

REMISSION

That's a big word. It means that the cancer
is all gone from my body. I will still have
to come to the hospital to see the doctors
and nurses to make sure the cancer is
not coming back and it is gone forever.

I like coming to the hospital. I get to play when I come into the Oncology Centre. The Oncology Centre is the cancer treatment room at the hospital. Just like the playroom, they also have so many toys and games here. The best part is that they have pictures of my favourite hockey player on the wall. His number is 16 and that's my birthday!

I have a favourite nurse and doctor; they are so kind and are always at the hospital when I come in. They show me where the secret treasure chest is. This is where I choose a toy after getting a needle. Getting needles doesn't hurt, it's just like getting a little poke in your hand or arm. Even though it can be scary sometimes, I tell all the other children I am strong and brave and that they are too.

I only have to come to the hospital once a year now. I'm sad because I do like it here, but I also know that it means that I'm getting better and better! My doctor and nurses need to help other children get better. They are the

SUPERHEROES

who made me feel so much stronger and will help all the other children too.

I am now a grown up and a Kindergarten teacher. I live a normal and healthy cancer-free life. All thanks to Children's Hospital.

I love Children's Hospital because it made me feel better and helped me fight the cancer out of my body. The hospital is going to help so many other children like me become a miracle child and help sick kids get better!

I'm now able to share my story about how strong
and brave I was during this hard time.
Just remember all children are

STRONG AND BRAVE!

How many of these butterflies did you see in the book?

Did you know:

"Butterflies are also a symbol of hope, joy and a transformation of change: meaning out with the old and in with the new. The same meaning a Stem cell transplant has for a blood cancer patient."
- Leukemia Cancer Society

CPSIA information can be obtained
at www.ICGtesting.com
Printed in the USA
BVHW020115090522
636264BV00004B/3